THIS BOOK
BELONGS TO

....

....

I can't tell you how grateful I am that you decided to read my book. My most heartfelt thanks that you took time out of your life to choose my work and I hope you find benefit within these pages.

There are so many books available today that offer similar content so that makes it even more humbling that you decided to buying mine.

Tell me what you thought! I am eager to hear your opinion and ideas on what you read as are others who are looking for a good book to buy. Leave a review on Amazon.com so others can benefit from your wisdom!

With much thanks.

©COPYRIGHT 2024

The content contained within this book may not be reproduced, duplicated, or transmitted without direct written permission from the author or the publisher. Under no circumstances will any blame or legal responsibility be held against the publisher, or author, for any damages, reparation, or monetary loss due to the information contained within this book. Either directly or indirectly.

Legal Notice:
This book is copyright protected. This book is only for personal use. You cannot amend, distribute, sell, use, quote, or paraphrase any part, or the content within this book, without the consent of the author or publisher.

Disclaimer Notice:
Please note the information contained within this document is for educational and entertainment purposes only. All effort has been executed to present accurate, up-to-date, and reliable, complete information. No warranties of any kind are declared or implied. Readers acknowledge that the author is not engaging in the rendering of legal, financial, medical, or professional advice. The content within this book has been derived from various sources. Please consult a licensed professional before attempting any techniques outlined in this book. By reading this document, the reader agrees that under no circumstances is the author responsible for any losses, direct or indirect, which are incurred as a result of the use of the information contained within this document, including, but not limited to — errors, omissions, or inaccuracies.

Table of Contents

Chapter 1	8
Why Your Team Is Failing	8
What happens to Organizations when teams fail	13
Chapter 2	18
Creating and Building a Team Using Howard Gardner's Theory of Multiple Intelligences to Build your team.	18
Making sure your team is working in their strength zone	24
Allow the team members to Invite their whole selves to work	29
Chapter 3	35
Do an Interest Survey	40
Placing people in their strength zones	42
KD Bradshaw quote: It's all about developing Rituals and Routines	46
Chapter 4	52
Articulate the Shared Common Vision	52
Empower your Team to do the Work	55
Reasons Why Business Communication is Critical to Your Company's Success	59
How To Make Good Decisions	64
Chapter 5	69
Be Clear about your Culture Organizational Climate and Culture	69
Prepare for your Team	72
Allow employees to give feedback and take sufficient action	76
Chapter 6	81
Unwillingness to build a hybrid or remote team	81
The challenges of having a hybrid or remote team	84

INTRODUCTION

No matter what you're selling, your business won't succeed without a fantastic team behind it. From the moment you bring on your first employee to the day your business opens its doors to the public, building an effective team can be one of the essential parts of making your business run smoothly and successfully. Getting off on the right foot with each new team member will give you the best chance of keeping them there for as long as possible.

One of the problems and pains an average entrepreneur goes through include having a team that needs your constant attention. Nothing gets done, or no deadlines are met without you pulling them along. Some are stuck with a few resources and keep asking you when they can finally bring some money into your business. Their skills, or lack thereof, drag down your productivity and make it difficult for you to meet goals. Some go along without a hitch, but others feel like they're treading water while waiting for direction. This can cause burnout and create a needlessly stressful work environment. And if one member of your team is unhappy, another is likely as well - which means you could lose valuable employees who will leave and hurt productivity and morale further.

Another problem is when you feel like your team is working against you. There is no shared vision and goals, No Buy-in. The roles in your team are either not defined or ill-defined. This is one of the biggest reasons why teams fail. There is a lot of frustration and wasted time. Also, some members do not commit and think their efforts won't make a difference. As a result, motivation dwindles over time, people become apathetic about what they are doing, and their contribution towards achieving goals becomes limited in the long run.

Lastly, if you feel the people you put in place are not living up to your expectations based on their potential. For example, you may have hired them because a friend or family member referred them. They might have been good employees at their last job, but they don't seem to be working out for you. So what do you do? Do you fire them and hire someone else? Or do you try to figure out why they aren't performing well and correct it? If so, how do you go about doing that?

This book will help you put systems in place for creating a team that is a well-oiled machine, where everyone is working in their strength zone and up to their highest potential. You'll learn how to hire people who fit into your company culture and build strong relationships with them, so they feel appreciated, respected, and valued. You'll also learn how to get them working together effectively so they are motivated and productive rather than frustrated or distracted by each other's work styles. Finally, it's time to stop wasting time trying to fix all of your employees' weaknesses - instead, focus on building on their strengths! In today's business world, we have access to more information than ever, but many entrepreneurs still struggle with hiring new employees or making changes within their teams.

Creating a winning team for every organizational task is one of the most important aspects of running a successful business. It is not only that will help you get more done, but it also will help you create a better business environment. Teams are responsible for building products, marketing them, selling them, servicing customers, and everything else. So if you want your business to grow faster than ever, you must learn how to build an effective team. This book contains proven steps and strategies on how to do so. You can choose any method or technique as per your convenience but make sure that they all work together to achieve your goal of building a great business empire.

James H. Bradshaw Is the right person to be writing this book because he has taught these strategies to others, and they have been successful in their endeavors. Teaching and leading for over 20 years made him an authority. He has his Masters in Educational Leadership. In addition, he is an entrepreneur who has developed several successful businesses.

Helping you create a high-value team matters deeply to him since what you're about to learn helped him build his business from just one to a team of people who value his vision and work toward their common goals with little direction or correction from him.

His experience makes him more credible in what he is teaching you. He knows what it takes to build a team, so you can trust that you will learn everything you need from him. The author is passionate about helping people succeed in life, which is why he wrote all of his books on entrepreneurship and leadership development. His passion comes through in his writing, making it easy for readers to understand his meaning when discussing business management or leadership skills.

Most people don't just wake up one day and decide to start a business. You start with an idea, but that's not enough to make it happen—you need funding, a business plan, solid marketing strategies, etc. In other words, you need help. With Business Leadership Uncovered: The Entrepreneur's Guide to Building and Maintaining a Successful Team, you get all that help and more! Each section covers crucial topics entrepreneurs must know to succeed—and no stone is left unturned. It is common knowledge that small businesses are America's most incredible success story—and with Business Leadership Uncovered as your guide from start-up through long-term growth, yours could be next!

Chapter 1

The Problem - Teamwork Doesn't Always Make the Dream Work

Why Your Team Is Failing

Teams are the fundamental building blocks of business, and every company relies on them to get work done. But why do teams fail? And how can we prevent these failures from happening? To help you overcome this challenge, we've put together this comprehensive guide on the top seven reasons teams fail and how to prevent them from happening.

Lack of trust

A lack of trust is one of the most significant factors in a team's failure. Before you can have confidence, you must first commit. Without commitment, there isn't trust—and without trust, it doesn't matter how committed your team is. The reason is that everyone (teammates included) will always make choices based on what they believe to be in their best interest, not necessarily what's in your best interest or your company's best interest. If you don't know what you want from each other or don't feel like each teammate understands their role, it'll be difficult for any level of commitment or trust to grow within a team. When teammates don't commit to one another, they only commit to themselves. They're not looking out for others' interests or even considering those interests when making decisions. Instead, they're just doing whatever is most convenient at that moment, with no regard for how it might affect anyone else down the road.

Ineffective leadership

Poor leadership can lead to team failure in multiple ways. Some leaders don't know how to effectively manage their employees, which leads to a dysfunctional environment that turns talented professionals into frustrated workers. Others may micro-manage a team, leading to communication breakdowns and unproductive outcomes. No matter what kind of leader you are, it's essential that you try not to undermine your colleagues or dissuade other employees from working with you. It takes time for people on your team to trust you, so work hard at building relationships early on. Take charge of your role, but leave space for others' ideas as well—and never forget that you need others if you want your project/team/company to succeed. Finally, don't make any assumptions about your ability to complete a task or achieve an outcome all by yourself. You might be great at what you do, but there is no I in a team. This is especially true when trying to accomplish complex goals requiring multiple stakeholders' input. Focus on getting everyone on board and contributing where they can; that way, everyone will feel invested in achieving success together (or avoiding failure).

Poor communication

Communication is a vital component of team development. When communication breaks down or doesn't exist, a team can't move forward; it will fall apart. As a leader, your responsibility is to ensure that each team member understands what they need to do to contribute. In most cases, you don't have time for long discussions on why something needs to be done or communicated in an email, chat message, or even over coffee; it has got to be concise with no room for misinterpretation. Team communication is just as important as individual communication because everyone on your team must understand exactly what each person is doing. Poor communication is one of the biggest causes of failure for any team. Don't let your team suffer from poor communication by putting these tips into practice:

- Start each meeting with a quick update about progress and check-ins regarding roadblocks.

- Set expectations early, so there are no surprises along the way.

- Meet regularly (weekly) to discuss new developments, address issues, and track progress.

- Take notes during meetings and document tasks/action items, so people are accountable for their work.

- Schedule regular 1:1s with every team member where both parties discuss goals, achievements, obstacles, or anything else relevant to their performance.

Lack of vision

A lack of vision in a team can lead to poor performance. Team members have varying goals, which can be problematic if not reconciled early on. Team members are less likely to succeed or impact their organization without a shared purpose. Before starting a new project or initiative, clarify your vision as a team so everyone knows the objectives. This could be as simple as writing out what you want your final result to look like and sharing it with others. It will give everyone a clearer idea of what's expected from them. If there is no clear vision for your team, it will cause problems down the road.

Lack of decision making

As a team member, take responsibility for making your voices heard and be involved in decision-making. Don't be afraid to ask questions or suggest alternatives. As managers, you must be clear about what decisions need consensus or input from all team members. When managers say, I've made up my mind, so there is no point in asking me any questions, it sends a message that they are not open to new ideas and don't want their team member's suggestions or opinions. This makes people passive as they feel it isn't worth raising their concerns if they will not be taken seriously. It also gives managers an excuse for making poor decisions! You can never improve your choices if you do not get feedback. So make sure that everyone has a chance to contribute, even if it is just by saying I agree with X rather than disagree with Y.

Lack of interest

It's pretty hard to have a team if no one is interested in being on it. Everyone has different interests, so make sure there's something in your project that will appeal to all your teammates. For example, if you are working with kids, try incorporating projects they are interested in. Think about what gets them excited, then find a way to get into that project! After all, they might not be interested in math at school, but if you use math skills to help design new toys or experiment with items around your house, they might like that! Another idea is to let each member choose their project for a week, then switch it off each week. This allows everyone to lead their group and explore things they may not normally do.

Lack of empowerment

Empowerment makes a great deal of sense from an organizational perspective. Organizations hope that everyone will be happier and more productive by giving staff a wide degree of freedom to make decisions within their remit. The trouble is, though, when people are empowered, they tend to become responsible for those decisions. It's only natural – we all want something we've invested time in achieving or creating ourselves. Then, we feel bad about it when it doesn't work out as planned. We blame ourselves. And our self-esteem takes a knock. However, if someone else had made those decisions for us, we wouldn't feel so bad about things going wrong – even if someone else was at fault! To avoid team failure caused by a lack of empowerment, you must ensure that your team members have responsibility without blame: they should have autonomy over their actions and protection against mistakes.

Conclusion

First impressions count. Remember that you're building a foundation for an entire company, not just a meeting. Be on time, dress appropriately, and respect everyone's time. When communicating with your team, remember that communication is vital; if they don't hear back from you immediately, they won't feel valued or heard. Lastly, understand that your team has its strengths and weaknesses; make sure to utilize everyone equally while also emphasizing areas where someone may need help improving their skills. Remember:

The goal isn't to find better people—it's simply not worth it—but to improve each team member so that they can become even better at what they do.

What happens to Organizations when teams fail

A leader's role has become significantly more complicated in recent years, with ever-increasing levels of accountability and expectations from the board of directors and stakeholders. One single employee can easily be the difference between success and failure in almost any company today, let alone an entire organization. And if your staff cannot work together effectively as a team, it's unlikely that you'll have much success leading them. That's why every leader needs to consider what happens to organizations when teams fail and take steps to ensure their business doesn't fall into the same traps as others before them.

Interpersonal

In a worst-case scenario, team members may lose their relationships with each other. Without civility, respect, and support, communication breaks down, and you lose one of your most powerful tools for getting things done. You also run into issues with employee engagement and shared responsibility—the entire reason for teams in your organization to begin with. When employees don't feel engaged or when they see others as adversaries rather than partners in success, productivity falls, and retention rates go up.

In today's competitive employment market, where too many candidates are vying for open positions, losing a good employee can devastate a small business because finding qualified replacements is increasingly difficult. And that means lost revenue and wasted time recruiting, hiring, and training new employees. When it comes to retaining talented employees, fostering an environment of teamwork is critical. First, make sure that employees understand how their jobs contribute to the bigger picture and what's expected from them at work every day. This way, they can have more impact on company goals while feeling like valued contributors who have control over their destinies within your organization. Then, promote teamwork by communicating with team members regularly about how individual efforts support organizational goals. The result will be greater employee engagement and higher morale – which equates to lower turnover rates! To create a culture of support, civilities, and collaboration among employees, start by focusing on what's right between people. Be mindful of personal attacks, divisive comments, and demeaning remarks. Instead, promote mutual respect among employees so everyone feels comfortable being themselves without fearing retaliation or exclusion from critical decisions affecting their careers and lives. That goes for managers and employees—when leaders practice healthy interpersonal interactions, it filters down your whole organization in ways that help sustain overall performance. At some point, all employees need support from coworkers to achieve career goals. Make sure they know how much you value them and their contributions to your organization so that they stay engaged with their jobs. A word of caution: if employee engagement isn't high enough, ensure not to mistake workplace politics for support. Workplace politics often masquerade as collegiality but can lead to even more significant problems, such as gossiping and spreading rumors behind someone's back (which has its own set of problems).

Once again, show employees that constructive criticism should always be delivered respectfully; otherwise, your words might fall on deaf ears. Even worse, some employees might use destructive criticisms as excuses not to do anything. This can be a real problem for organizations, especially in fast-paced environments where timeliness and efficiency are crucial. Employees need to trust that they'll receive constructive criticism promptly and that you'll address their concerns quickly. Team members sometimes rub each other wrong no matter how hard you try to prevent situations from escalating. It happens. When it does, take immediate action to minimize any damage before your team loses faith in your ability to support them. Remember that no matter how great your vision is for your organization, nothing gets accomplished without teamwork. Your employees play a significant role in determining whether your organization thrives or flounders—so keep their needs in mind as you consider different strategies for building employee engagement and boosting morale.

Innovation

If a group of people with different skills or ways of thinking collaborate, it can lead to new and creative ideas. But if a group doesn't work well together, it creates an environment that stifles creativity. When that happens, valuable knowledge is lost; a team may be unable to develop and share information from one individual to another—leading to a lack of learning opportunities. If employees aren't sharing what they know and can do on their own, their overall value at work will suffer. Collaboration has its benefits, but teamwork also has its downfalls. For teams to succeed in today's business world, they must balance cooperation and creativity. It takes creativity to generate new ideas, but collaboration keeps those fresh thoughts alive by spreading them around.

The bottom line

When a team fails, everyone loses. And we all lose when teams don't work together effectively. As a result, innovation stalls, productivity and efficiency take a nosedive, talent retention is harder to achieve (because people will leave if they don't want to work with their teammates), and division takes over a company as factions are created. The best way to avoid these problems is by ensuring teams operate at their highest level—which begins with hiring decisions. Great organizations employ great people who fit into cohesive groups working toward one goal: success for your organization. It doesn't matter how smart or talented your employees are if you don't have cohesive teams. Hiring a bunch of high-powered superstars may even hurt you in the long run because you won't be able to get them to play well together! Instead, start with building cohesion and trust among your employees and watching innovation skyrocket. It's not only possible; it's inevitable when teamwork wins!

Studies repeatedly show that organizational performance suffers when a team fails. And from an employee's perspective, working in an incohesive environment can lead to job dissatisfaction and disillusionment with an organization. Unfortunately, many factors are involved in determining whether or not an executive team functions well together. Factors range from individual personality traits (like social introversion/extroversion) to group dynamics like competing between members or sharing knowledge within the group about an upcoming project before other members know about it. To combat some of these issues—particularly interpersonal conflicts between coworkers—the most important thing is to create open lines of communication, so everyone feels comfortable sharing what's on their mind without fear of reprimand. After all, how can you resolve problems if you don't talk about them? There's no magic bullet for building cohesive teams; every situation is different. But as long as you're aware of potential pitfalls and take proactive steps to avoid them, your chances for success will be much higher!

When individuals work better as part of teams—and when those teams function optimally—productivity skyrockets, time wasted on side conversations is minimal, and lines of communication stay open. On top of that, innovative ideas are easier to come by when more people have input into various decisions because they're more invested in them! Ensuring your company hires quality candidates who mesh well will help create cohesive teams that deliver high-performance results for your business. Teamwork may be one of the essential qualities you look for when hiring new employees, so consider how these candidates interact during interviews and determine if they'll be able to work together effectively once hired. When teamwork wins, everyone wins!

Conclusion

Teamwork is essential to effective organization and efficiency, but when team members don't work together effectively, problems arise. All members of an organization need to know how their efforts contribute to a larger vision. Teams can begin to break down when individual agendas outweigh a shared vision. To help maintain order and cohesion, develop strategies for your team that ensure each member is working towards achieving your company's vision and mission. Keep lines of communication open so that any issues between members can be quickly resolved before they turn into significant rifts; treat disagreements as opportunities for growth and improvement; implement systems to encourage positive behavior and engagement; reward success with individual contributions. By taking these steps, you'll be able to avoid falling into fractions and division within your team.

Chapter 2

The Mindset - A Valued Team will Always Bring the Most Value

Creating and Building a Team Using Howard Gardner's Theory of Multiple Intelligences to Build your team.

In 1983, Howard Gardner proposed his theory of multiple intelligences, suggesting that traditional notions of intelligence - linguistic, logical-mathematical, and spatial - are not the only kinds that exist in the world. Instead, he proposed that musical, bodily-kinesthetic, interpersonal, intrapersonal, and naturalist intelligence contributes to people's success in life (Gardner, 1983). The following content describes how you can use Gardner's theory to build an effective team in your organization or business today.

Visual-Spatial Intelligence

Characteristics include high spatial reasoning skills and the ability to visualize mental images. They are typically good at finding their way in large organizations or seeing things others may have missed.

Strengths include being able to visualize models of a project before they act. Potential Career Choices: Designers, sculptors, painters, artists, architects, police officers (find hidden clues), mathematicians, engineers. People with high levels of visual-spatial intelligence can find their way easily around unfamiliar environments, create mental maps of unknown places, and picture how various parts of a system will fit together.

Linguistic-Verbal Intelligence

If you are strong in linguistic intelligence, you have a keen ability to organize information, express yourself verbally with words, and learn languages. As Gardner notes, there are two significant characteristics of people with high linguistic intelligence: First, they have little difficulty finding words for thought. They have a wide range of synonyms for everyday objects. This characteristic relates to their second quality: They enjoy playing with words. Students with high linguistic intelligence include poets, professional comedians, lawyers; journalists; speechwriters; diplomats, public relations specialists, and teachers - especially English teachers or language instructors. You can identify children with high verbal intelligence by their performance on multiple-choice tests that measure meaning or sound instead of rote memorization or naming.

Logical-Mathematical Intelligence

If you are strong in logical-mathematical intelligence, your strengths could include high academic achievement, a knack for numbers or science, and detailed organization. To put these strengths to use in business, turn your eye toward technical roles such as bookkeeping, budgeting, accounting, or research. Logical-mathematical thinkers are also frequently skilled at problem-solving, planning, and paying attention to detail; these skills will help you succeed as a manager or leader. In addition, organizations may rely on logical-mathematical thinkers for their ability to find solutions that can be expressed in facts and figures. This type of thinker often makes decisions based on data, which is why they tend to do well in jobs where they have access to information and can base decisions on those findings. The most common careers for logical-mathematical thinkers include engineering managers, accountants, statisticians, and mathematicians.

Bodily-Kinesthetic Intelligence

Your strengths lie in building things with your hands. You have incredible motor skills, which means you can perform difficult feats quickly. While not necessarily correlated with creativity, bodily-kinesthetic intelligence is often a good predictor of artistic ability—such as dancing or sculpting. If art isn't your thing, bodily-kinesthetic intelligence is also a key strength among athletes (think of Michael Jordan). You're probably good at sports, exercise, or any form of physical activity that requires skill and speed (you should try figure skating!). Like any strength-based approach, using your abilities as part of a team-building process will only be effective if all parties are willing to play their strengths. This intelligence represents your potential for self-understanding and empathy. You understand yourself well but may struggle when dealing with other people. Your internal self is constantly evolving and growing; so are your values and goals.

Musical Intelligence

People with high musical intelligence have exceptional pitch, rhythm, and melody. They often have perfect pitch or excellent relative pitch. Musical intelligent people are typically tuned to lyrics, melodies, beats, and harmonies. They make lovely musicians, composers, producers, and recording engineers. Successful careers in these fields may include studio musicians, jazz musicians; music arrangers; songwriters; singing coaches; electronic music creators (DJs), record producers, radio station executives, broadcast technicians, live sound engineers, and lighting designers. Real estate appraisers may also use their musical intelligence when evaluating the property for purchase. They can make great salespeople, too. Their natural affinity for music allows them to listen carefully to what is being said to quickly pick up on any underlying meaning that others might miss. When they talk about your product or service, they'll say things that will help you gain customers' trust and show you how your product solves a problem that no one else has figured out before.

Interpersonal Intelligence

An Interpersonal Intelligence team will make you a better salesperson, marketer, or any other role that relies on external relationships. The best way to build relationships is through social interaction, so those who excel in Interpersonal Intelligence are natural networkers who seek out new connections. Strong interpersonal skills make for strong leaders since developing others is one of your core strengths. Gardner calls interpersonal intelligence the ability to understand others' feelings and perspectives. With strong interpersonal skills, you can anticipate your audience's needs and concerns before they even have them. For example, suppose you speak passionately about something you believe in (because your business exemplifies that). In that case, customers respond positively because they feel they can trust you with their questions or concerns. Personal Intelligence focuses on identifying your strengths and weaknesses. Those who are self-aware tend to be good communicators and listeners, which makes sense given that being aware of yourself helps you communicate effectively with others. Your job as a leader is to motivate your employees, which means being able to clearly articulate what everyone should be doing every day at work.

Intrapersonal Intelligence

Understanding your strengths, weaknesses, personality type, etc., can be crucial to building a solid foundation for your relationships. To have a good relationship with yourself is one thing—you need self-awareness to achieve that—but if you're interested in having successful relationships with others, intrapersonal intelligence is an important starting point. Being aware of where you succeed in certain areas, what interests you in life and how you want others to perceive you will not only help you understand yourself but also give insight into how others see you. That understanding can help prevent negative conflict or awkwardness that can crop up over time because of miscommunication. In addition, having strong interpersonal skills can help you develop long-lasting, healthy professional relationships. In business settings, intrapersonal intelligence means being able to recognize your strengths and weaknesses while simultaneously identifying those of others on your team (or who might potentially join). For example, you may know how you prefer to work best or what situations tend to make you uncomfortable, but figuring out these things about everyone else on your team will ultimately benefit everyone involved.

Naturalistic Intelligence

Each intelligence has a different set of characteristics that describes how people operate. For example, Naturalistic Intelligence has a strong sense of conservation, living in harmony with nature. People who have a high potential for Naturalistic Intelligence can recognize many features or characteristics in things around them, such as plants, animals, or natural phenomena. They have keen senses that help them interpret their surroundings more accurately than most other types of intelligence. These individuals are often very good at identifying objects, even if they have never seen them; therefore, they tend to be gifted with an innate understanding of animals and plants. This is one of Howard Gardner's original eight multiple intelligences. It is associated with strength in areas like artistic talent, perception, intuition, and appreciation for beauty. Individuals who excel in using these skills may pursue careers as artists, writers, or photographers because they can put their imagination into tangible form through words or images.

The Mindset

Knowing about the multiple intelligences can be extremely helpful when it comes to hiring and building a strong team. It will save you time and money. It will help you to understand your team members better. It will help you know what positions to fill. Case in point, if you have a team with three different types of intelligence on it you might want to hire a fourth type to round out the team. This is not to say that a person can't have two or more types of intelligence. However, knowing this is super helpful when building a successful team. This is because all people have different strengths and weaknesses, and by understanding the different types of intelligence, you can better identify what each person is good at. Furthermore, you can create a more well-rounded and successful team by catering to people's strengths. It's one thing to just get a person working but if you can get them working passionately in their strength zone; you have accomplished something! So if you're looking to build a strong team, don't forget to consider the many faces of intelligence!

Someone who is musically intelligent would have different strength zones than someone who is logical-mathematical intelligent.

Knowing which intelligence your candidate falls within makes it easier to know if you need that person on your team. This will also help you put them in their strength zone. For example, musically intelligent people would probably do better with marketing or creative projects. On the other hand, someone who is Logical-Mathematically intelligent would work better with budgeting and accounting tasks. The goal here is to find out what the best place for each person would be so they can use their natural strengths while they are working.

Making sure your team is working in their strength zone

Unfortunately, not all of us have the same strengths. Yet many of us work in situations where we feel we're overqualified, underused, or just plain out of our element. Suppose you're stuck in this situation and feel frustrated or dissatisfied with the job. In that case, it may be time to rethink your working environment and consider whether there's another position that would suit your needs (and strengths).

When to use your superpowers

You might have one or two core competencies at work, but the odds are that you have more. We're always happier and more productive when we use our strengths—so how do you figure out which ones they are? It turns out that a lot of us don't even know what our strengths are. A strength assessment like Gallup's Clifton StrengthsFinder can help shed light on your natural abilities and talents. Once you know your strengths, it's time to set up an environment that allows you to bring them into play daily. Doing so is key to being successful professionally. If you're having trouble finding ways to use your strengths, consider using these tips.

Identify your strengths

It's a simple concept: Identify your strengths and focus on them. Sounds like common sense, right? And yet it is astonishing how many people fail to do just that. We often get sidetracked doing what others want us to do—or what we think they want us to do—instead of doing what comes most naturally. We forget that strengths are those things that come quickly or flow. So any time you struggle with a task, take a step back and ask yourself if it falls into one of your identified areas of strength. If not, why not? Is there another way to attack it so that you're utilizing your skills and gifts? How would someone else tackle this project which had different strengths than you?

Determine what you are naturally good at

Identifying and leveraging your strengths is one of the most important things you can do to be more productive. Studies show people perform best when they are working with what they are naturally good at, so try to determine what your strengths are and work to leverage them—especially in a professional setting. Here's how: write down all of your typical tasks during a typical week; then, next to each job, list two or three words describing your most vital skill or attribute for completing that task. For example, if you were writing about an upcoming meeting with a new client, you might put a client presentation on your list. Underneath it, you might write organization and creativity. This tells us that organization is something you do well (and may even enjoy), while creativity may not come as quickly to you but could be a strength if developed further. You should also consider which of these qualities are transferable across different situations—in other words, will they help make other tasks easier?

Use your strengths every day

This is a significant source of our greatest joys and successes. We're naturally motivated by what we do best, which gives us energy. This strength zone thing isn't new or revolutionary—it comes from more than 100 years of applied psychology research. If you can identify your talents and use them every day, it will change your life. You'll be happier, healthier, and more successful. You have to put yourself out there to get started! You don't need to figure out everything at once; take baby steps towards success. Find one small way to apply your strengths today, and then build on that tomorrow. Before long, you'll have all kinds of ideas for making things happen for yourself! Your unique combination of talents and skills will help you stand out from everyone else, so let your strengths shine! It shows when you feel good about who you are and your actions. And people respond positively to those who are confident, capable, and comfortable with themselves. Remember: Confidence doesn't mean being arrogant or conceited; it means feeling good about yourself so that others feel good about you too.

Understand other people's strengths

You need to know how other people work best as a business owner. And that means understanding their strengths. Most leaders focus too much on weaknesses instead of capitalizing on another person's strengths. 90% of leadership development training focuses on what people do wrong rather than what they do right—and it's no wonder that only 10% of employees report being actively engaged with their organization. Instead of wasting time on someone else's weaknesses, focus your efforts on helping them succeed by deploying and building upon another person's strengths! A leader who understands how other people work best allows everyone to perform at their highest level, leading to more substantial results!

Pick tasks you can ace with ease

Before you start your tasks, spend a little time thinking about what you will work on. Choose something well within your strength zone, and don't try to tackle an item beyond your current skill level. This could be where professional help might be helpful; a mentor or colleague could steer you away from assignments that will take longer and require more energy than necessary. Remember that energy is key, so make sure you're working on tasks where your effort will yield solid results instead of spending time trying to fix mistakes caused by inexperience. Also, remember not to overwhelm yourself with too many projects at once; small steps often produce better results than giant leaps forward when it comes to project management.

Narrow down the list of tasks

When you're overwhelmed with a huge to-do list, sometimes it helps to focus on one thing at a time. Try narrowing down your list of tasks and prioritizing them by importance. Focus on just one job and eliminate distractions like phone calls or meetings that aren't critical, then work on completing that task before moving on to another. By focusing on only one study at a time, you can zero in and complete it successfully. You might even get more done than usual because you're not wasting time switching between different projects. Narrowing down your to-do list allows you to use your strengths for each project rather than trying to do everything equally well.

Break the task into manageable pieces

Sometimes, procrastination can be a matter of not knowing where to start. Figuring out what you need to do (and then doing it) often requires some momentum. Break down big projects into manageable steps and get started. Once you've broken a large project into manageable pieces, create short-term deadlines for each step. You may even find that once you've started a project, other related tasks come to mind and are easier to accomplish. The best way to break tasks down is to focus on creating with your strengths instead of your weaknesses; we all have our strengths, so why waste energy? For example, if writing isn't one of your strengths—don't start by trying to write a book! Instead, try creating an outline or begin by brainstorming ideas. Or, if public speaking makes you uncomfortable—don't give a speech at an event! Instead, volunteer to introduce speakers or ask questions during Q&A sessions. By working within your strength zone and focusing on starting small rather than being overwhelmed by tackling everything at once, you'll feel more motivated and productive when it comes time to work on more significant projects.

Do something different for a change

Your productivity will plummet if you continue to work at your current pace, even if it's a pace that allows you to get things done. Some signs indicate you're ready for a change: You always look tired and stressed; you never have time for exercise; you don't feel like doing anything but work; and so on. To boost your productivity, do something different from what you did before or learn a new skill. Go up or down the market, or try a new platform or device. For example, an accountant who has been focusing on tax returns may be more productive switching to payroll and administrative tasks for other businesses. And an insurance adjuster might find he's more productive handling claims with another company with fewer gray areas than his former employer-provided. If you don't want to switch jobs, there are other ways to break out of your rut. Take classes online, attend workshops and read books about related topics (but not during work hours)—set goals for learning something new every quarter. Whatever changes you make, do them slowly enough that they won't threaten your job security. Remember: If nothing changes, nothing changes! Be patient as you give yourself time to explore different possibilities—and remember how much better you'll feel when you've regained control of your career!

Allow the team members to Invite their whole selves to work

Everyone has the best self and an authentic self. Most of us are at our best when we can use both at work, according to Gallup, Inc., an American analytics and advisory company based in Washington, D.C. The most engaged workers bring their authentic selves to work every day, learn something new and are fully present at work. At the heart of employee engagement lies the ability to get your whole self to work and be recognized as an individual by your employer and co-workers (Gallup, 2020). Here are some tips on how to make this happen.

Why Employees Should Bring Their Whole Selves to Work

According to psychologist Martin Seligman, Emotional well-being is more than just good moods; it also includes a high energy level and engagement. Your day-to-day happiness at work can be attributed partly to your attention—how absorbed you are in your career and how much you care about its success. When you're fully engaged, says Seligman, a positive feedback loop of positivity kicks in (Seligman, 2011). The more energy and interest employees bring to their jobs, the better they do; their increased productivity leads them even more absorbed and engaged. And studies show that when people get their whole selves into work — not just their skills or credentials — they have higher satisfaction with life and work. For example, one study found that emotional well-being was twice as important as job security and pay in predicting employee engagement. So if you want to improve employee engagement at your company, start by encouraging everyone to bring their whole selves to work. That means helping them understand what makes them unique, so they feel comfortable sharing those parts of themselves with others (and letting go of any fear or anxiety around doing so). It also means creating an environment where authenticity is valued and encouraged — one where people feel safe taking risks and being vulnerable because they know there's support from leaders, colleagues, friends, and family members.

Befriending Co-workers

Your co-workers are more than just people you happen to be working with. They're your allies under challenging projects, your companions on late-night shifts, and your mates when everyone else is out celebrating at that office holiday party. Your relationships with co-workers matter, however close or casual they may be. A 2014 study of workers at a Midwestern manufacturing plant found that relationship quality was linked to how much employees liked their jobs and how well they thought they were doing at them. Stronger relationships mean better job performance—meaning it pays off personally and professionally for you to become an engaged friend who knows what's going on in his co-workers' lives. To do so, start by asking questions about your colleagues' personal lives: How are things going? Are you having fun? What have you been up to lately? If there's something wrong, ask if there's anything you can do to help. And don't forget: You're friends outside of work too! Keep up those friendships by taking time to hang out outside of work, whether grabbing coffee together or planning a night out at a happy hour.

Understanding Your Management Style

There are many different ways to approach management. First, managers must be aware of their management style and how it affects employees. If a manager is not comfortable with their management style, it may be time to reevaluate what works best for them and their team members. To understand your management style, you should self-reflect on how you interact with others and how people view you at work. Think about past experiences at work when you have: felt appreciated, respected, understood, and trusted by employees; had trouble getting your message across; felt embarrassed or humiliated by others in front of others; had difficulties working collaboratively with others; found it difficult bringing up conflict with people in a professional manner. These situations can help determine what management style will work best for you and your team. You can also ask colleagues who have worked with you to describe your leadership strengths and weaknesses. Try to get honest feedback from as many people as possible so you can genuinely see yourself through their eyes. Once you know where your strengths lie, try to develop other areas that need improvement.

Finding Common Ground between Co-workers

When you are engaged at work, there's no denying that your work becomes more enjoyable. But engaged employees don't just feel happier—they perform better and stay longer, too. To get your colleagues engaged at work, it's essential to understand what motivates each employee and how you can help them find common ground with their co-workers. After all, every person has unique needs; employee engagement isn't about creating a cookie-cutter approach for all employees. Instead, each individual has unique personality traits, experiences, and working styles that will inform what type of engagement tactics resonate with them best. The key is understanding who they are as people and helping them bring their whole selves to work.

Bringing your whole self-drives innovation and well-being

If you have doubts about bringing your whole self to work, consider that a new study from KPMG shows what employees already know. The top reason for employee disengagement is not having an opportunity to use their strengths in their jobs. In contrast, engagement increases by 31% when people use their strengths at work; they are 43% more likely to be innovative and 50% more likely to feel engaged with those around them. But how do we get there? How do we become involved? It's pretty simple: bring your whole self to work. We've identified seven areas where most of us tend to hold back our true selves and how leaders can help create cultures where each person feels safe taking risks and expressing their authentic self daily. For example, many women don't speak up as much as men because they're afraid of being judged or criticized—which can lead to fewer opportunities and less recognition. And while some might think it's easier for extroverts than introverts to express themselves authentically, introverts have a unique challenge: They need time alone after social interactions to recharge before doing it all over again. So if you're an introvert who likes quiet time alone, make sure you carve out some space between meetings, so you don't wear yourself out! Or if you're naturally outgoing but struggle with saying no when others ask too much of your time—well, maybe it's time to say no!

Setting Boundaries with Teams and Colleagues

One of the most valuable skills you can learn as a manager is setting boundaries between yourself and your team. This helps you maintain your sense of well-being and makes it easier for you to support and care for your team members. In particular, setting limits on time spent outside work together helps ensure that professional and personal lines aren't blurred. Be firm about what time spent together qualifies as work-related, so there's no question when too much time has been spent socializing at work events or getting lunch together. When mixing with co-workers turns into excessive after-hours texting, it can quickly become gossiping or complaining —things that have no place in a healthy office environment. Setting clear boundaries around these activities will help everyone feel more comfortable.

Establishing Inclusive Communication Lines

Employees at all levels of an organization need to have a voice. Encourage open communication by being approachable and actively listening, ensuring you create positive relationships with team members across all positions. Communicate with purpose: Don't be vague or lazy in your communication with your team members; do so meaningfully. This will help ensure they are on board and engaged in tasks when it comes time for assignments or next steps. Make feedback a two-way street: Allow employees of any level (even entry-level) input on changes or suggestions they would like to see implemented within their role, department, or company. This allows them to feel included and gives them ownership over their work. Finally, provide opportunities for growth: Employees who feel challenged and valued tend to stay longer than those who don't. Offer ongoing training opportunities, promote from within whenever possible, and ensure room for advancement in every position.

Chapter 3

The Practice- If you Build it, They will Come

If you have an idea that you think would be successful, the worst thing you can do is nothing and wait to see if it takes off on its own. Many entrepreneurs make this mistake—they think that if they build it, the people will come, and they'll succeed automatically. The fact is that you have to take action and market your product or service to attract an audience and get sales and customers in the door.

Picking the right people

Hiring the right people to work in your business is one of the most important decisions you'll make as an entrepreneur, and it can have a lasting impact on your company's success or failure. As such, it's essential to follow some steps to hire the right person, but there are also some common mistakes you must avoid if you want to hire the best candidate. Check out these tips on hiring the right people for your business!

Assess your company's culture

Your company's culture can either attract or repel top talent. If you want great employees, you have to provide them with an environment they enjoy and one that aligns with their values. When hiring new staff, interview candidates in person instead of over e-mail. Use a process like Holacracy to ensure all new hires is held accountable to company goals and that they will thrive in your workplace environment. By taking these steps, you'll be able to identify which potential employees are best suited for your organization. You can then train them on what it takes to succeed at your company before officially bringing them on board.

Create detailed job descriptions

Hiring is one of those things that can be both exciting and scary. With such a significant expense, creating an open application and a detailed job description with specific responsibilities and expectations is essential. Asking candidates how they would accomplish each task or assignment listed in their job description will help you see how well they understand your company's expectations and fit within its culture. It's also essential to make sure that you don't just ask questions like Tell me about yourself or what are your strengths? While these questions provide some helpful information, they're very general and easy for applicants to answer in a way that makes them look good on paper but doesn't necessarily mean they have what it takes in real life.

Where to look for candidates

If you're launching a new start-up or trying to fill an important position at your current company, reach out to friends, family, and colleagues first. If you're struggling with a particular role—say sales—ask contacts in that industry which headhunters they like working with. You can also post job listings on Monster and Craigslist or use social media channels such as LinkedIn and Facebook. LinkedIn has become more valuable than job boards for some businesses, particularly creative agencies because it's where their target candidates are likely to be spending time. But don't rely solely on these tools: Get out there and look for potential hires yourself! Attend events and meetups related to your field, especially if you're looking for someone with expertise in something specific. Also, consider local networking groups; depending on the business you're starting, several relevant groups may be nearby. The point is: Don't just sit behind your computer waiting for candidates to come to you; get out there and find them!

Test

You'll need employees no matter how large or small your business is. But, as much as you may want to create and run a 100 percent do-it-yourself enterprise, some core competencies are better off outsourced—at least at first. This test will help you figure out what roles would be best served by an outside party, how to find those candidates, and how much to pay them. Complete it when you feel ready and revisit it as soon as possible; we're sure there will be questions or sections of information that don't apply in six months but might apply now.

Prepare well-structured interviews

One of the biggest reasons bad hires are possible is poor preparation. Before you even consider advertising a job opening, consider what kind of person you want to work with you. Are they going to be hard workers? Are they organized? Do they like pets? Have they worked at a similar company? Would they like to work in an office environment or prefer something more free-form and creative? Once you have some idea about what kind of person might fit best into your organization, it's time to move on to preparing your interviews. Remember that nobody likes interviewing - if you can make their job more accessible, the chances are that hiring will go much smoother for everyone involved.

Interview questions you should ask

What are some of your strengths? What are some of your weaknesses? Where do you see yourself in five years? What type of work environment motivates you and why? What activities do you enjoy outside of work, and how do they contribute to your success at work? Why did you leave previous jobs/careers (even if it was only short-term)? How would a close friend or family member describe you? On a scale from 1–10, rate yourself on leadership, problem-solving, and analytical skills. If we offered you a job today, what is one thing that would make or break that decision for you? What are three positive traits about you? Tell me about a time when you successfully managed multiple priorities. When have you been most satisfied with your performance? Tell me about an accomplishment where you've exceeded expectations, even though it wasn't part of your job description. Tell me about a time when something didn't go as planned and how you handled it? Describe a time when something didn't go as planned and someone else needed to clean up after you left. Tell me about an important goal that required long hours over several months—how did working toward that goal impact other areas of your life like health, relationships, etc.? What can I expect from our first day together on the job?

Look beyond the CV

If a CV looks suspiciously like every other one on your desk, that's a sign that you're hiring based on qualifications, not personality. A little difference can go a long way in today's highly competitive job market. So when it comes time to recruit new team members, don't be afraid to take note of non-standard academic backgrounds or life experiences – being different from everyone else could also mean being precisely what you need. And if someone sounds too good to be true, think twice before making an offer: talent isn't always visible at first glance. There are plenty of candidates who employers have overlooked in favor of more conventional applicants. Hiring managers may dismiss them as too weird or inexperienced, but they might be perfect for your company.

Ask for references

A job reference can be a good indication of a prospective employee's values and character. If you have time, put together a short list of questions about skills, personality, and professional history to help you make an informed decision about who to hire. It may also be helpful to look at some references in advance (ideally via e-mail) so that you know what types of questions to ask when you meet with them in person. It's essential not only to check references but also to ensure they're happy with how they were contacted and promise they won't get contacted again unless there is something more relevant or urgent. This way, references aren't inconvenienced or annoyed by unrelated follow-up calls or e-mails. It would be best if you also permitted potential employees to contact their references independently before hiring new hires. Having them reach out to those contacts first will save you from getting those same people later. Plus, it shows your new hire initiative and responsibility—two things employers are always looking for in their staff members. And finally, if all else fails, use Glassdoor: it has both company and employee reviews, which means a candidate has likely been asked similar questions before (which means they will probably answer honestly).

Bring them onboard

It's essential to hire not only someone you like and trust but also someone who is a good fit for your needs. Make sure they know how long they are needed and if there will be any additional responsibilities later down the road. Also, don't forget that great employees are self-motivated, so let them know they can come to talk with you if they have any questions or concerns. Finally, when it comes time to take things further and add another employee, remember that these new hires should mesh well with those already on board; their personalities should fit everyone else's (think about team building here). Also, make sure their skills are a good match. In addition, don't forget background checks. You never know what skeletons might be in someone's closet.

The point of all these steps is to avoid hiring too quickly because you're in a rush. You want to find quality people that fit well into your company's culture and vision. And while finding just one person may seem easy enough, making sure they're doing everything correctly. Take time to do yourself a favor and look at more than one candidate before deciding on one! Hiring slowly allows you to get as much information as possible from each person without rushing through interviews. Once you've found an ideal candidate, consider offering them an employment contract. This document outlines expectations for both parties involved and helps establish a formal relationship between employer and employee—which can be helpful when things get complicated.

Do an Interest Survey

Are you always trying to fix your weaknesses instead of accentuating your strengths? The problem with this approach to life is that it's slow, hard work, and it can be demoralizing if you don't see progress quickly enough. So instead of getting bogged down in what's wrong with you, use these three assessment tools to find out what makes you uniquely strong and unique!

Personality Type

There are many different personality assessments, each intended for a specific purpose. For example, some are geared towards helping you get along better with others (the DISC) or measuring your potential for success in particular jobs (the 16PF). Of course, the best one for you depends on what you're trying to accomplish. Still, as a general rule, tests that focus on your top five or six strengths tend to be particularly helpful—two options worth considering: The Five-Factor Markers or VIA Character Strengths questionnaire. Learn more about these tests and others in our write-up here. Once you have your results, look at them carefully and consider how they might help guide your career path. Ask yourself: How can I use my strengths to achieve my goals? Where can I learn more if I have no strengths in a particular area? What new skills do I need to develop? How can I leverage my existing skills?

The DISC Model

We have a few suggestions if you're unsure where to start when it comes to identifying your strengths. The DISC model—developed by psychologist William Moulton Marston in 1928—is one of our favorites because it can be applied across various contexts. It breaks down people into four main categories: Dominance, Influence, Steadiness, and Conscientiousness. These are typically paired with these descriptive adjectives: Decisive, Excitable, Accommodating, and calm (which could also be referred to as Diplomatic). Determining which adjectives apply most strongly is simple enough: think about yourself for a few minutes and jot down how often each trait applies. Then you can use those descriptors to help determine which category might fit best. For example, if you write excites more than once or twice, then Influence might be a good fit. Once you've identified your dominant category, try thinking about how they affect your life daily. For example, if decisiveness is your strongest trait, then that's what others see first and foremost in their interactions with you; if calm were a strong point for you, that would likely influence others' perception of who they're dealing with given time.

Strengths Finder 2.0

A simple, free online test that identifies your top five strengths. Once you find them, you can use various tools and exercises to develop those strengths. Plus, a free workbook is available to record and keep track of your progress. If you're interested in learning about how your colleagues rank their strengths, many companies offer workshops based on Strengths Finder or other similar tests. Of course, there are various reasons why assessing your strengths is essential — we already mentioned career development. Still, it can also help improve job satisfaction and increase happiness at home. So get started today! The test takes less than 10 minutes to complete.

Placing people in their strength zones

Everyone has an area of expertise and an area where they are the weakest. Great leaders and managers worldwide know how to put their employees, colleagues, and direct reports in their strength zones. They have learned how to recognize it and how to get the most out of everyone on their team by putting them in that zone.

Why We Need Leaders

It's common knowledge that people don't leave companies; they leave managers. In other words, leaders can make or break a company. Most leaders are promoted because of their expertise and ability to lead teams and projects—but there's a difference between leading on a project and leading an entire team. So how do you know if you have what it takes to be a good leader? It starts with understanding your strengths so you can put others in their comfort zones. Great leaders understand their strengths and weaknesses, as well as those of their employees. Then they assign tasks accordingly. By knowing where each person excels, leaders give themselves a better chance at success—and boost morale by ensuring employees use skills they enjoy using every day. So here are some questions to ask yourself: What am I good at? Am I organized, logical, and detail-oriented? Do I thrive under pressure? What about my employees: Are they good communicators, problem solvers, and self-starters? Once you identify these qualities (or lack thereof), start assigning tasks accordingly. For example, if someone is strong in communication but not problem-solving, consider giving them one more verbal task than a written task each week. Not only will you encourage them to use their strengths—you'll also find out which ones need more attention. You may even discover that specific jobs aren't suitable for certain people.

The Best Way to Lead

One of today's hottest leadership trends is a framework known as strengths-based leadership. In short, strengths-based leaders believe that employees are more productive when doing work that fits with their innate personality traits, strengths, and styles. Instead of focusing on improving weaknesses, leaders help their teams capitalize on natural abilities to achieve higher performance and tremendous success. This can be done in many ways, such as taking inventory of skills and placing each person into a strength zone— an area where you excel and add value to your organization. For example, some people may be gifted at systems thinking while others have an eye for detail; some exhibit excellent communication skills while others enjoy working independently. The key is identifying what makes people tick so they can thrive in roles that match their strengths.

Strengths are Key

Most of us don't have time to think about our strengths and what we're good at. (Life is hard, after all.) Even when we take a minute to consider our strengths, it can be easy to get stuck there—to think about ourselves as only our strengths rather than as people with diverse experiences. But when leaders look beyond a person's strengths and growth opportunities, they help team members reach their full potential at work. For example, you might assign someone who is typically creative and bold a project that requires organization and accuracy. In doing so, you provide an opportunity for them to try something new while tapping into past talents. As a result, your employee will gain experience in skills they may not have previously considered. And by giving your employee a chance to stretch outside his comfort zone, you are helping him grow and become more valuable over time.

Giving people opportunities by putting them in their strengths zone

Great leaders know how to utilize people's strengths instead of asking them to try and do what they're not good at. You don't have to be a sports coach or military general to put people into their strength zones. In business, placing your employees in roles where they can excel makes for highly engaged, happy employees and a team that works well together. When you consider their strengths as well as the role they play on your team, it creates better efficiency and consistency at all levels of business. By identifying and leveraging each person's unique talents, you have a much better chance of building a team that will be successful on its merit—and a much higher chance of having happy staff members who are eager to achieve company goals. The most important thing is to make sure everyone knows what their strengths are so they know where to apply them most effectively. And by providing opportunities for those individuals with clear objectives and measuring success against those objectives, you create an environment of mutual trust that leads to engagement. That's why aligning people's strengths with their job responsibilities are so important: if we get our A-players doing what they're best at, we're going to win more often than not. That doesn't mean we shouldn't work on improving weaknesses—we should—but we need to find ways of compensating for those weaknesses until our players reach a point where they can address those issues themselves through training and practice.

Developing your strengths

Everyone's strengths are different. That said, we all have them; it's just a matter of knowing what they are and making them work for you. You can do that through self-awareness, which is challenging but critical if you want to be a good leader. Having an innate grasp of your strengths means being honest about who you are—not where others think you should be. In reality, no one can know what will motivate or challenge another person as well as that person does (and there will always be differences). So how can you find out your strengths? Start by writing down what motivates and challenges you. Then ask people who know and care about you (maybe even your manager) what they see when they look at your performance.

Finally, consider taking a personality test like Myers-Briggs or DISC to gain insight into what makes you tick. Remember: There's nothing wrong with having weaknesses. Just be sure not to try and fix things that aren't broken!

KD Bradshaw quote: It's all about developing Rituals and Routines

KD Bradshaw, the founder of The Productivityist, says that developing rituals and routines can help eliminate distractions and increase productivity (Bradshaw, 2018). Creating rituals—or specific actions you take daily or weekly—helps guide your behavior so you're more productive by default. Plus, once you start this new habit or pattern, it's easier to continue doing the same thing each day because it doesn't require any extra mental effort. For example, you might develop the ritual of setting aside an hour every morning to work on an important project before checking your email or getting distracted with other tasks.

Introduction

To develop good life habits, you must be consistent with your efforts. Habits are nothing more than routines that we perform at least three times every week. Once these become a routine, they're easy to stick with because they're not a change in your lifestyle. They are just a way of life now. It takes 21 days to form a new habit, so if you can figure out how many days per week you want to implement them (Monday through Sunday, for example), it makes it much easier to make them part of your weekly schedule. If my goal is three or four daily habits, I know that it will take 70 or 80 days until they become routine and easy as pie! The key here is consistency.

You can't expect to do something for 30 days and then give up because it gets tricky. You have to keep going even when things get tough. This applies to all areas of your life, from eating healthy to exercising regularly to saving money. When you're able to develop a positive habit, you feel great about yourself when you accomplish your goals, and seeing yourself improve over time will motivate you even further!

What are Rituals?

A ritual is an established routine or pattern of behavior. It can be a repeated daily activity, such as getting up at 7 am every day, having a shower every night before bed, or jogging after work. Some everyday rituals are: drinking tea/coffee in a certain way; eating your favorite meal at your regular restaurant when you don't feel like cooking; spending 10 minutes before sleep reading a book; playing a relaxing instrument once you get home from work. Doing these things at set times on specific days eventually become habits (which we'll talk about below). Most people have 3-4 extensive rituals that help them manage their mood and reduce stress throughout the week. Having rituals also means you're more likely to stick with good habits because they become part of your routine. You won't need to rely on willpower alone! I think it's essential for everyone to have some daily ritual because it provides structure and a sense of calmness in our lives. If something terrible happens during the day, it feels much easier to deal with if you know what will happen next – rather than just dealing with whatever comes next without any preparation. Having routines also makes life easier because you know what will happen each time something occurs (e.g., someone asks for help, there is an argument, etc.). This reduces anxiety by providing us with certainty about how we should respond!

Creating rituals can be challenging but rewarding

It's challenging to carve out time for rituals when life is busy. We know it, but we still have to make time. This is why they are so rewarding. They help us take a step back from life to appreciate what matters most, either by reflecting on what has gone right in our day or making time for someone else in our lives who needs it. It's hard to re-prioritize our lives, especially if there are dozens of competing priorities vying for our attention daily, but creating rituals helps us prioritize ourselves and others healthily. In addition, it's a way of ensuring we don't forget what matters most each day as we get distracted by other tasks or daily obligations that may not seem as vital as they are. Sometimes, all we need is a reminder. Sometimes, all we need is to put things into perspective. And sometimes, all we need is just five minutes alone with no distractions to refocus our energy where it belongs. That's what rituals can do for us: keep us focused on what matters most while also helping us find peace on even our busiest days.

The power of sharing your ritual with other people

Researchers have found that if you form a habit, you should identify a keystone behavior—and activity that links several good practices together. Some routines might already be part of your daily life. For example, you probably brush your teeth every morning or do some work out on most days, but those activities are independent. What if you could link these behaviors? For example, brushing your teeth could trigger a shower and then (as long as it didn't take too long) some journaling before bed. Over time, forming good habits becomes easier because you don't have to think about them as much since one behavior triggers another. This makes starting new habits easy. So, how can you develop a routine like this? It all begins with ritualizing your everyday activities. A ritual is an established pattern of behavior that people engage in repeatedly to achieve a specific goal. So if you want to create better health habits, you might try ritualizing exercise, so it happens first thing in the morning, right after breakfast. This will make working out into an ingrained pattern for yourself, and eventually, it will become a normal routine—so regular that it'll seem silly not to exercise first thing every day!

Introducing ritual into your life

A ritual is any routine activity, physical or mental, that has meaning in your life. It can be as simple as brushing your teeth every morning before work. Or it could be a weekly girls' night out with your best friends. The key is that it's an activity you do regularly because you choose to, not because you have to. Regular habits in your life give your day a comforting structure that sets you up for success – whether that means managing stress better, boosting productivity, or maintaining good health (including physical fitness). Pick at least one ritual and commit to practicing it for 21 days to see how much of a difference it makes in your life! Here are a few ideas to get you started: Exercise regularly: Commit to doing some form of exercise three times per week. This could mean running in the morning, doing yoga after work, or playing tennis on Saturday mornings. No matter what form it takes, find time each week where you're active on purpose rather than passively watching TV or checking Facebook. Next, take time each day for self-care: Take 10 minutes in the morning and 10 minutes at night to give yourself time and space. Please make sure these moments are free from distractions like email, social media, and other responsibilities, so they're genuinely my time. Finally, create a gratitude journal: Every evening before bed, write down three things that went well during your day and why they went well.

Adding routines to your life is another way of creating habits

Take a cue from habit expert BJ Fogg, Ph.D., director of Stanford University's Persuasive Technology Lab. In his paper on cultivating healthy habits (PDF), he lists several strategies for adding routines to your life:

- Set the alarm to go off at a particular time

- Give yourself something you have to do at a particular place at a specific time—e.g., floss after brushing your teeth

- Create external accountability by telling someone what you will do each day

- Use apps that can track and measure your behavior (Fogg, 2019)

While these tips are geared toward health-related behaviors, they apply just as well to work-related ones. So try setting reminders in your calendar or using a tool like RescueTime to track how much time you spend on various tasks throughout your day. You might be surprised at how much more productive you are when accomplishing goals if you keep them top of mind all day long!

The next step is developing rituals around those goals. For example, if one of your daily goals is writing three pages in your novel every morning before work, then make sure that getting up early enough to squeeze in those three pages becomes part of your routine.

Routine can help when you have anxiety or depression

Getting into a routine allows you to establish a steady rhythm to your day, which can help you feel better. For example, if you can, get out of the bed regularly every morning—even if it's just to get dressed or read in your room. It might not sound like much, but it can start helping you develop structure in your life and improve your mood over time. You should also find ways to make relaxing a routine activity as well. For example, try taking warm baths at night or going for a walk after dinner on weeknights. These little habits will help you learn how to calm down when things aren't going well so that they become more accessible when they do go wrong. If you don't have any calming routines already, start trying some new ones today! You may be surprised by how much they help.

Chapter 4

The Dive in - Building Your Team with the Right Mind

Articulate the Shared Common Vision

All great organizations, from sports teams to charities to your company, have one thing in common: everyone in that organization knows the shared vision and believes in it wholeheartedly. Your company will only ever be as good as its shared vision, so it's essential to put time and energy into creating the right one for your group of people. Use these steps to make the shared vision you need to succeed in all aspects of your business.

Start with something compelling but practical

Make sure you choose something that's personally compelling. You may have to spend some time thinking about what it is, but if you come up with something that gets you excited and motivates you personally, it will inevitably be passed on to others. Avoid buzzwords: Many businesses avoid saying what they do because they're worried that competitors can use their description as ammunition. It's true: If you write we are an advertising agency, your competition could technically use that description against you if they set up shop and call themselves an advertising agency. But remember that if someone wants to compete with you for customers, chances are they already know what type of business your business is anyway! Don't fret; there's little value in protecting from imaginary threats. Use clear, concise language: Remember that potential customers aren't coming to your website or reading your content because they want to read a marketing textbook. They want information—precisely information that helps them solves their problems. Keep everything short and easy to read so readers can get to those solutions quickly. Don't assume everyone knows what you mean: Just like avoiding jargon isn't just about preventing confusion (it also shows you respect your audience), avoiding acronyms isn't just about keeping things simple (it also shows you respect your audience). When writing copy, always assume people don't know what every acronym means—and spell out any acronyms immediately, so people don't have to look for definitions elsewhere on the page or site.

Cultivate vision ambassadors

Every member of your organization should be able to understand and articulate your vision. They should also feel that they are integral players in making it happen. Help them get there by helping them see how their daily actions affect broader objectives, like building an excellent customer experience or keeping up with demand. The key is not to have everyone sing the same hymn but to ensure they're all speaking (and acting) from a shared platform. Constantly reinforce how each person can contribute by doing their job exceptionally well, ultimately serving as fuel for achieving vision goals. Here are some ways to create ambassadors who believe in your vision:

- **Don't just talk about it; live it** - A big part of being a great leader is walking your talk. Whether you're a CEO or department head, demonstrate what being on board looks like through every interaction and decision you make.

- **Set a strong example** - Remember when teachers would give kids an example problem to solve at home? Doing so was good practice and clarified what success looked like—making it easier for students to replicate that success on test day.

- **Be open to questions** - When people ask questions, they don't fully understand something. Asking lots of questions isn't always easy, primarily if you've been tasked with leading a group of people or departments. However, if someone asks why you did something or wants more information about something related to your vision, take advantage of that opportunity to clarify expectations and explain how things work together.

- **Be accessible** - Leaders need to know where their teams stand at any given time, whether one employee is reporting back after conducting market research or ten employees providing feedback after receiving new training materials.

Create checks and balances

Creating checks and balances among your decision-makers is one of the most important things you can do for your company. You need people checking each other's work, not trying to persuade or hurt one another. If done right, checks and balances help assure that actions are taken with careful consideration and fairness. Ultimately, they help create accountability within an organization—which is critical when executing your shared vision. Who will be accountable for making sure new accounts come through? How will decisions be made? What happens if a decision isn't executed correctly? These are all questions you should have answers to before creating any plan. Make sure everyone involved has buy-in before moving forward.

Empower your Team to do the Work

In today's economy, empowering your team members to do their best work is more important than ever. However, to get the most out of your employees, you need to provide them with the right tools and freedom to get the job done without over-management or micromanagement stifling them. These five tips for increasing empowerment in your team will help you do just that.

Delegate responsibility

If you want to increase your team's empowerment, you can start by giving them more responsibility. Studies have shown that employees feel most empowered when given autonomy over their work and decision-making. To increase empowerment in your team, assign tasks to specific members of your team rather than having everyone work on everything. Also, leaving room for employees to make decisions regarding how a project is completed—from which tools are used to what style guides are followed—will go a long way towards increasing their job satisfaction and motivation. If an employee has questions or suggestions, encourage them! This will help encourage them to try new things and seek feedback that may help improve their performance. Ultimately, empowering your team will lead to better collaboration and higher productivity.

Have trust in your team

Trust is a crucial part of a healthy team. You won't get much done if you don't trust your employees or they don't trust you. Get to know your team members, help them grow as professionals and colleagues, and show them that they can make decisions on their own. You might even come to rely on their strengths—and they might be better at making certain decisions than you are! When everyone has confidence in everyone and feels like they can be themselves, it creates a great work environment where everyone is more engaged and motivated. This means greater productivity, which is a win-win for you and your team.

An excellent place to start building trust with your employees is with small interactions:

- Thank them regularly.

- Ask about their personal lives outside of work.

- Take an interest in what they do when they aren't working with you.

Give autonomy

Giving your team autonomy over their work may seem scary, but it's a critical factor in motivating people. People have to feel like they're doing meaningful work to feel like they're contributing something important to your organization. You can give people that sense of purpose by letting them take ownership over their projects and initiatives and ultimately decide how things get done. Encourage individual growth: Nobody is good at everything, so encourage your team members to grow into roles they aren't traditionally trained or comfortable with. If you don't challenge them, how will they succeed? You'll help employees gain confidence and become more engaged with their jobs by allowing them to learn new skills. Invest in training programs, offer opportunities for side projects outside work hours or hire an outside trainer if necessary. Provide feedback regularly: Employees need regular feedback to know where they stand with their performance—especially when learning new skills and taking on new responsibilities. Schedule time each week (or month) to check in with each team member about what they are working on now and how they feel about their progress toward goals. Communicate clearly: The more clearly employees understand what's expected from them, the better equipped they are to deliver results.

Show appreciation

No matter what you do, there will always be people who agree with you and those who don't. Instead of throwing your energy into trying to change their minds, put that energy into showing appreciation for what they do agree with. When they start agreeing with more and more things, they'll become less inclined to disagree out of principle alone. This creates an environment where it becomes easier to explore new options in a collaborative spirit because no one person feels like another individual's plan is pressuring them. Even if everyone on your team isn't passionate about a project, try putting yourself in their shoes and looking at their situation from an empathetic perspective instead of asking why they aren't excited about something. You might find that even though they don't think much of it now, they may come around to appreciating some part of what you are doing after some time has passed. A little patience can go a long way toward making empowerment happen!

The best way to get anything done is to make it so easy that they have no choice but to say yes. Start with small requests first and then move up from there. The path of least resistance is usually easiest for both parties involved, which means your employees will feel empowered when you ask them for help. The chances are good that over time, as trust builds between everyone involved, empowerment can begin naturally without any direct requests on your part.

Focus on results

There's an easy way to test whether your team is empowered: ask them. You're on track if employees believe they have absolute authority and are free to achieve results. But if you find their answers always end with I can't do X because Y, you may need to take a closer look at your methods. If part of your job as a manager is to distribute responsibility, make sure your people know what's expected of them—and that they know you trust them to get it done. Employees who feel micromanaged won't be engaged in work or company goals. Instead, empower them to succeed. This means setting clear expectations and providing resources (both monetary and human) for getting work done. Once you give your team more freedom, give yourself some credit, too: allow others to use their creativity without micro-managing every step of progress (or lack thereof). Finally, remember that not all solutions will come from within; if needed, seek out mentors or coaches who can help push past any stumbling blocks.

Reasons Why Business Communication is Critical to Your Company's Success

Communication is one of the most significant issues in business today and has been since the beginning. If you can successfully handle communication with your clients, employees, vendors, family members, and friends, you will be on your way to success with anything you do.

What Are the Different Types of Business Communication?

You should be aware of five different types of business communication: external, internal upward, internal downward, internal lateral, and public. External communication happens when you communicate with an outside source; think clients or customers. Internal upward communication includes all your messaging from employees to upper management. Internal downward communication is similar but moves in reverse. Internal lateral communication involves collaboration between departments and teams on a particular project or goal. Finally, public communication happens when you have something you want to get out there that isn't necessarily work-related; it's simply a part of your brand. Determine which type(s) of communications are most crucial for your company's success so that you can streamline them for efficiency and clarity across all departments and teams. Here are 11 reasons why communication is critical to your company's success.

Improves employee engagement

In today's global market, it's essential that your staff stay connected and invested in your business. Improved communication allows them to feel like they're part of what you're building. According to a recent study conducted by online collaboration tools provided by LogMeIn, 68 percent of remote workers are more likely to feel engaged at work when they can communicate easily with their co-workers, compared with 47 percent who said they felt engaged when they had no access at all. Making sure your team has a platform for communication also enables you to make better hiring decisions: Remote workers have access to candidates' technical skills and personalities, which ultimately leads companies toward making better hires overall. In addition, this improves collaboration within teams and ultimately leads to higher-quality work for clients.

Eliminates email overload

Good communication within a company can help eliminate unnecessary emails and keep team members up-to-date on what's happening. For example, when you know your co-workers are working on an assignment with similar goals, it can save you time from asking what they're working on or double-checking that they got everything they need. It also helps streamline meetings, so essential topics aren't discussed multiple times. Overall, effective communication will save your company time and headaches.

Eliminates communication silos

Regular communication with your colleagues allows them to share their insights, which helps your team avoid relying on anyone. If a colleague spends a week in another department and picks up on a new idea or process, that's great—as long as he shares it with you when he returns. When people feel isolated from their colleagues, they cannot contribute outside their job description, which can harm your business. Instead of worrying about who knows what and keeping everyone in the loop, encourage collaboration through regular meetings and email threads. With these tools in place, you must listen—your team will do all the work for you!

Increases employee productivity

It has been proven that business leaders who have a regular communication schedule with their employees report more excellent employee retention, satisfaction, and productivity. According to Forbes magazine, one hour per week in time spent on communication can generate an extra $100,000 per year of revenue. In addition, when employees feel connected and know what is expected of them, they are more likely to contribute to their fullest potential. Conversely, without regular business communication, your employees feel less connected and much less productive; this can be detrimental to your company's growth.

Improves inter-departmental communications

If there's one thing that good business communication does, it's bridge gaps. It brings people together and helps them share their knowledge and ideas. Business communication helps foster a unified understanding of a company's direction, said Dan Strom, founder of Panoramic Consulting, a San Francisco-based business consulting firm. It's impossible not to experience communication breakdowns when departments aren't communicating on common goals. Without good communication between departments, employees in your company will fail to work towards shared goals because they lack insight into what those goals are in the first place. Good communication can help fix these issues before they cause any significant problems. And poor communication skills can be just as damaging within your company as outside of it.

Improves communication with remote workers

Remote workers play a significant role in many businesses these days, but a big challenge that faces companies that rely on remote teams is how they keep everyone on track. So put, most of them don't. For some reason, communication between remote employees can be tricky and even more challenging to manage than if they were all in one office together. The critical issue with remote employees is that it's harder for a boss or another co-worker to step in and correct a case when a problem arises because there aren't any visual cues. They're not sitting next to each other, and their voices are coming through their headphones instead of surrounding them physically.

Reduces employee turnover

Employees who feel appreciated and supported have a higher job satisfaction rate, leading to less employee turnover. And when employees leave your company, it can cost you money – in terms of both what you lose in productivity and what it costs to hire and train new workers. When employers invest in improving communication between them and their workers, they lower employee turnover rates.

Improves knowledge-sharing efforts

If too many cooks are in one kitchen, it can be challenging for business teams to share knowledge effectively. When communication lines aren't clear or don't exist at all, valuable information never gets disseminated. And that means your employees miss out on crucial insights they need to drive growth and success. The best way to maximize knowledge-sharing efforts is by encouraging everyone on your team — from management down — to ask questions, learn new things and share what they know as frequently as possible. Writing a weekly email blast highlighting a recent project milestone or sharing notes with colleagues at a company-wide meeting are great ways to facilitate information exchange. It's not just about actively sharing information; it's also about identifying sources of important data so you can efficiently communicate it across the organization when needed.

Increases employee advocacy

Everyone in your company needs to communicate consistently, concisely, and effectively with customers. Whether you are an employee or CEO, you should be reinforcing good communication behavior throughout your company. By developing clear expectations for what it means to communicate well and holding each other accountable, employees will build trust within their relationships with customers. In addition, employees with an established communication method that aligns with customer expectations will feel more empowered to do their job well and learn from past mistakes.

Improves customer satisfaction and retention

Well-executed internal communication fosters understanding, reduces dissatisfaction, and builds a strong foundation for customer satisfaction. Dissatisfied customers are rarely satisfied by receiving more information, primarily if that information doesn't directly address their issue or come from someone they trust. When employees don't understand something (or don't feel they have enough authority), they communicate poorly with external customers. Poorly communicated business rules mean unhappy customers who may churn—and expensive re-acquisition costs. When employees trust each other and feel empowered at work, it directly impacts customer experience and satisfaction. This shows in better reviews, fewer support tickets, and phone calls about your product or service. And happy customers spend more money with you over time!

Builds a better company culture

Good business communication can strengthen a company's culture, improve employee satisfaction and retention, and prevent churn from bad bosses or job environments. At times in our lives, we may wish for actual loner status, but very few of us get through life without having to interact with others. Internal lateral means speaking directly with those around you within your company. An internal downward communication flows from supervisor to employee so that employees feel free to bring up concerns about workplace conditions or their performance. Internal upward communication allows employee feedback on how management policies are affecting workers. These are all ways companies create an open environment where all stakeholders feel like they have a voice and are heard in decisions at every level of the organization.

How To Make Good Decisions

The ability to make good decisions—and to do so quickly—is one of the defining attributes of great leaders and managers, but the truth is that making good decisions isn't always easy. Whether you're considering hiring a new employee or deciding how much to raise prices on your products, several factors can influence your decision and make it more challenging to choose one course of action over another. That's why it's crucial to build your decision-making skills from the start, especially if you have any plans of getting involved in management at some point in your career.

Identify your overall goal.

Business leaders face a million decisions in a day. It's essential to keep your eye on your overarching goals and focus on taking action. In other words, make another one. If you take enough measures and make good decisions, over time, you'll be better off than if you tried to sit down and analyze every decision point-by-point. And don't forget that even bad decisions have their place; by identifying mistakes quickly, you can use those experiences to help inform future decisions! What are some of your favorite methods of making quick but informed decisions?

Evaluate the significance of a decision

We don't get to choose what happens to us in life, but we do get to choose how we respond. That being said, it's essential that we learn from our mistakes and that we don't let a single decision define us. Mistakes make significant learning experiences, so long as you take advantage of them and recognize their significance. Many entrepreneurs have pointed out that making a wrong decision is often better than not deciding. When faced with an important business decision, consider your options carefully and ask yourself if it will lead you closer or further away from your ultimate goal. If you keep these points in mind, you'll be able to make good decisions without letting your ego become involved too much. And who knows?

List the positives and negatives.

As you consider a decision, it's essential to list all of its positive and negative attributes. You can see how it will impact your team, your company, or your career by having a complete list of pluses and minuses. This creates an objective assessment that is free from overhype or negativity. Ultimately, it allows you to make a quick decision based on your knowledge and own it. No worries—you can learn from it next time if it's a wrong decision. And remember that rapid success is not always the best; slow and steady can win the race in business and life.

Revisit your decision

The first step in making good decisions knows your options. If you're having trouble with a decision, chances are other options are available. Look at your prospects again and evaluate them more closely, then pick one. When it comes to business decision-making, nobody likes being wrong. But if you haven't learned from your mistakes, how will you ever make better decisions? If a decision doesn't work out as well as you had hoped, that doesn't mean it was necessarily a wrong decision—or even you made a mistake. Instead, learn what went wrong and why; that way, things will improve the next time.

Follow your instincts

Instincts can be wrong, but they are often right—and far better than over-analysis. Follow your instincts and consider input from others as they inform your instincts. But ultimately, make a decision. You'll know it was made in good faith if it turns out to be wrong. Admit you don't have all the answers, ask what you don't know, and then make a quick decision based on that knowledge. Own up to it if it is a wrong decision and move on. Recognize that making mistakes is part of learning to manage people—it's OK!

Do a cost-benefit analysis.

Before jumping into a new decision, it's essential to weigh your options. One way to do that is with a cost-benefit analysis. In its simplest form, a cost-benefit analysis includes three steps: Identify costs, identify benefits and compare each side. The best part about cost-benefit research is that you can do it on anything – big or small- no matter what's on your plate. So if you're considering buying a new set of golf clubs, start by asking yourself how much you paid for your last collection, how often you play, and how long it took until they were completely worn out (cost). Then consider why you play -- is it because of social opportunities? Love of competition?

Set time limits

One of KD Bradshaw's best quotes—and advice—is that decisions are reversible. Execution is not. There will be times when you're faced with multiple choices and only have a limited amount of time to make one, so instead of getting paralyzed by choice, set a timer and pick one when it goes off. You can always change your mind later or adjust your decision based on additional information. The key is to start moving forward. If you get bogged down in analysis paralysis, then nothing gets done. The faster you move forward with a good decision, the quicker you can start executing it and learning from any mistakes. This takes practice and requires some quick thinking (especially if someone else sets your timer), but once you get into a rhythm of making quick decisions and owning them, things become much more accessible. And who knows? Your initial gut reaction might even turn out to be right!

Consult with others

Even if your gut is right, don't be afraid to consult with others. Chances are someone else has had a similar issue and might have even tried dealing with it differently that may work better than what you've come up with. The key here is to find people who will give you honest advice that won't put their interests ahead of yours but will help you do your job better and provide valuable insight from their own experiences. Some companies have formal feedback systems so people can submit anonymous comments about co-workers; be wary about being too open here, as it could lead to backstabbing or bullying. If you think an individual manager or co-worker isn't doing a good job, you should talk to them directly. If they don't change their ways after talking with them, it might be time to go higher up on the chain of command. It's important not to let your emotions get involved—you need to make decisions based on facts and experience (and not just because you like someone). Finally, keep an eye out for future opportunities by asking yourself, what if? Questions (for example: What if I started my own business?). You never know where these types of questions will take you! You should always look at things from multiple perspectives before making any big decisions—don't just rely on your own opinion alone.

Refer to your past decisions

Part of becoming a good decision maker realizes you are only human. The second part understands that every decision you make creates a ripple effect. Because of that, you need to be prepared to deal with those repercussions when it comes time to make another one. If your first choice is not possible, try to find an option that closely resembles your first choice instead of settling on something lesser simply because it was available at that time. Making decisions in life requires a plan, and by planning, then giving it some time, you can always go back if necessary and revisit what works or doesn't work and adjust as needed. Then repeat that process until perfection!

Chapter 5

The Development - Preparing for and Understanding the Team you want

Be Clear about your Culture Organizational Climate and Culture

Organizational climate refers to the general emotional or psychological environment that permeates an organization; it influences employees' behavior and attitudes, influencing organizational climate and culture. Culture is defined as the shared beliefs, values, and behaviors of an organization's members that can be used to guide its actions and shape its future (Hess, 2007). Organizational culture exists within an organizational climate, which can positively or negatively affect organizational culture. Therefore, changes in one area of an organization (climate or culture) will affect the other.

What is climate?

It's not just something that happens outside but also refers to internal situations in an organization. You may have heard of organizational climate or organizational culture. Both terms refer to how people see themselves in their organization, their sense of trust or mistrust toward their immediate supervisors, and whether they feel they are a part of something larger than themselves. In his book Good Boss, Bad Boss: How to Be the Best and Survive The Worst, author Robert I. Sutton says that while organizational climate can be changed through skillful management, we cannot simply make it happen through decisions or new policies alone because it is based on human interaction (Sutton, 2010). The good news? This means you have more control over your employees' perceptions of their work environment than you might think. Here's what you need to know about organizational climate and culture to create a positive one for your business.

Key aspects of organizational climate

Organizational climate is a term that describes how employees perceive their workplace. Some of these perceptions are based on objective characteristics of an organization, such as pay, benefits, hours worked, or job security. Others are more subjective and result from leadership style or employee involvement in decision-making. We'll focus on employee satisfaction with aspects of their jobs, for example, pay and promotions, feeling empowered at work, general satisfaction with working conditions, opportunities for advancement etc. Organizational culture goes beyond employee satisfaction to describe shared beliefs and values among employees about what matters most to them in their jobs. It also refers to common practices in how people do their jobs and relate to one another. The key question here is whether employees feel like they can trust each other; whether they believe it's important to put team goals ahead of individual goals; whether they feel motivated by company goals rather than just personal gain; whether they understand why decisions are made and who makes them; whether they feel respected by managers even when those managers aren't being nice all the time.

Creating a positive climate

It's important for people to feel valued in their roles and for them to be emotionally connected to their organizations. Creating a culture that encourages staff members to contribute positively to organizational success is one of your most important leadership responsibilities. Demonstrating appreciation when employees go above and beyond is just one way you can make employees feel valued. Here are some other ways to create a positive environment where employees can contribute their best: – Encourage open communication by fostering relationships based on mutual trust and respect. Employees will likely be more productive when they know they can talk openly about any issues. – Listen to your team suggestions. Doing so will give you valuable insight into how things work in practice, which will help you identify areas for improvement and growth opportunities. You might also discover that what you thought was an issue isn't an issue! – Recognize employee contributions regularly through public recognition or private thank-you notes or emails. People thrive on being recognized for good work—and it doesn't have to cost much money or time either!

Establishing an effective organizational culture

The most important aspect of your business climate is that it should support employee development. It would be best if you created a culture where your employees will be happy and learn, grow, and develop as they advance their careers with you. There are several ways to make sure that everyone on your team is getting a lot out of their experience at work:

Hire people who fit into your organizational culture

Promote employee training

Encourage constructive feedback. If you want to build an effective organizational culture, these three things must be part of your plan.

Prepare for your Team

No matter how successful your business is, growth is inevitable. To continue to see strong performance, you must prepare your team to handle the additional responsibilities of growing a company, including hiring new employees and improving processes. This content will provide eight steps to prepare your team for the future while streamlining current operations so that growth doesn't hinder productivity. You'll find tips on ensuring your new hires are fully equipped to hit the ground running, introducing automation into your processes, and much more! Let's get started!

Define Your Goal

Before preparing your team, you need to know what you're preparing them for. As a leader, you must have clarity on your goals and always keep them top of mind. Ensure that your whole team is aligned and consistently working towards these goals. How will they know when or if they should grow if not? Defining your goal is a critical first step in preparing your team for growth. You can break down long-term and short-term goals into quarterly, monthly, weekly, and daily tasks. By setting a clear path forward that everyone understands, you'll be able to easily identify what your next steps are whenever there is an opportunity for growth.

The 5 P's: It might seem common sense, but preparation makes everything easier. As part of your preparation process for growing your team, make sure you think through each one of these points: Purpose: Why does growing our business matter? Plan: What will we do next? People: Who needs to be involved? Priorities: What comes first? Procedures: How will we accomplish our goals? Remember: there isn't just one way to accomplish any goal; be creative!

Set Clear Metrics

It's important that, as a leader, you set metrics for your team. Each team member should know their expectations and how they will be evaluated. For example, if your company goal is X number of customers by March 1st, 2018, then each department manager should have a picture of how their department contributes to those numbers. Please ensure everyone on your team knows how they are being measured and what is expected, so no one falls behind. This will make planning and executing easier for everyone. It will also keep things running smoothly when growth does happen because everyone is clear on their role.

Establish an Onboarding Process

The number one way to make sure your new employees are set up for success is by establishing a detailed and documented onboarding process. Think of it as a recipe; you have all of these ingredients (training, tools, and teammates) that must be blended just right to produce a good outcome (talented employee). The problem with most onboarding processes is that they are either too heavy-handed or not documented enough. Either way, it usually takes longer than expected and sometimes results in resentment on both sides. Make sure your employees feel like they have resources at their disposal, and then let them do their job! Of course, it's easier said than done but trust me, if you spend time doing anything during a growth spurt, it should be investing in your people.

Build a Support Structure

It's important to ensure you have a support structure before your business takes off because it's not uncommon for entrepreneurs to feel isolated or burnt out. You don't need to surround yourself with a ton of other entrepreneurs. Just find someone who you can trust and be honest with—someone who will give you an objective perspective on your situation. And remember: Having an effective support system may be more critical when things are going well than when they aren't. As psychologist Adam Grant writes, it's not that success blinds us to our flaws; success magnifies them (Grant, 2013). So look for people with whom you can have difficult conversations about what you're doing well and what areas could use improvement. Don't be afraid to ask for help if one is needed.

Show Them the Way Forward

Some managers are better at delegating responsibilities than others. Some are fine with tasking employees with a job and a deadline, and others are interested in mentoring their staff members' career paths. If you have younger or newer employees who have some potential, it's worth taking an active role in helping them get to where they want to be professional. Not only will it make them feel better about themselves and your organization, but it also allows you to coach your team—and keep them focused on key priorities along the way. Let's talk about how you can help prepare your team for growth.

Don't Forget a Good Sendoff

Even though you might be growing your business, it's important not to forget about your current employees. When a company is rapidly expanding, leaders sometimes forget they must give their workers opportunities. This can lead to unhappy workers who take their frustrations out on customers or look elsewhere for opportunities. If you're looking at increasing profits and growth, start by giving opportunities and recognition to your current team members. They deserve it! A quick shout-out to some of your employees with some kind words and praise could go a long way toward making them feel valued—and could potentially mean better customer service. Studies have shown that when workers feel more satisfied with their jobs, they are more likely to provide positive customer experiences. It makes sense: happy people generally make other people happy too!

Measure Performance and Adjust as Needed

Measure your team's performance. Then measure it again. Keep measuring it until you have clear insight into what works and doesn't when trying to achieve specific goals. This will help you decide whether or not changes need to be made and, if so, what those changes should be. Ultimately, when managing a team through growth, you want everyone on board with your vision—but that means they need to understand their role in helping achieve that vision and how everyone else's role helps them reach their individual goals. If there are any disconnects between those two things, now is a good time to address them before they become bigger problems.

Celebrate Successes

The easiest way to demotivate people is by telling them how they're not doing well enough. Instead, recognize employees' achievements, even small ones, and celebrate them. When you praise your employees' successes, you make them feel good about themselves and their work and motivate them to keep working hard and stay productive. A successful business is one where everyone knows their specific responsibilities and actively contributes to reaching company goals. Keep your team focused on its successes by celebrating each time a goal is met. That way, if an employee feels like they aren't getting recognized for his contributions, it won't be because of a lack of effort on your part. As a manager, you should understand that your job is more than just giving orders and pointing out when someone makes a mistake. It's important to realize that managers aren't supposed to do all the work—they're supposed to manage those who do! If you have employees who can handle tasks without being told exactly how every step should be done, don't treat them as incompetent; instead, encourage them to come up with new ideas for making things better and easier for everyone involved. Every member of your team has unique strengths that can benefit both you and other members of your staff. Encourage teamwork among all levels of workers by encouraging collaboration whenever possible.

Allow employees to give feedback and take sufficient action

Employee feedback can be a goldmine of information and insight, especially if you can implement it into your company's culture. Although incorporating employee feedback might seem like an overwhelming task, these five tips will show you exactly how to allow employee feedback so that it benefits your business as much as possible. The more informed your employees are about their needs, the better they'll be able to perform their duties and the happier they'll be with their jobs. This, in turn, will translate into positive word-of-mouth advertising, which will benefit your business immensely.

Incentivize

One of your priorities should be finding ways to ensure you get all the feedback and information you need. Incentivize employees by offering them rewards (pay, bonuses, etc.) for participating in internal surveys or other feedback initiatives. Tip 2: Make it easy: Another key has an open culture. Make it as easy as possible for your staff members—particularly those in high-level positions—to feel comfortable with giving feedback. Set aside a certain amount of time each week where everyone can share their thoughts so that everyone has a chance to speak out without fear of being singled out or reprimanded. And don't forget about nonverbal cues; it's also important to have some way for people to give anonymous feedback. Tip 3: Investigate and act on data quickly: The quicker you respond to employee complaints, concerns, or suggestions, the more likely they will trust you. Plus, if any issues need fixing right away—like anything related to workplace safety—you want them resolved as soon as possible before they become bigger problems. Investigate data quickly but carefully; you don't want anyone at risk of getting hurt because someone didn't follow up on what could have been a minor issue in hindsight.

Offer Anonymous Feedback

Removing an employee's name from criticism makes it easier for them to be candid. If you can't ensure anonymity, at least ask them to share any positive feedback they may have as well—many managers find that hearing both sides of an issue helps them make better decisions. When in doubt, ask yourself if you would be willing or able to tell your employees what they're doing wrong face-to-face. If not, consider adjusting your method of feedback. How Do You Want to Measure Success? This is another critical component of setting goals. Be specific and determine how you want to measure success to know when something has been accomplished. What will constitute a win? If there are no consequences for failing, then why try? Make sure that every goal is clearly defined and easy to measure, and use benchmarks along the way, so everyone knows how close (or far) a project is from completion. A clear definition of success also makes it much easier for employees to recognize failure before things get out of hand and turns potential setbacks into teachable moments. There's a big difference between falling short on a goal and flat on your face!

Have a regular check-in point

If you want employee feedback, you must ensure it happens regularly and consistently. People need time to consider their answers and don't always have time during work hours. By scheduling an official feedback check-in point, employees know when they'll be expected to give input. Additionally, it will build trust if you allow them to say whatever they think without retribution. They should feel like they can be open and honest even if it doesn't make them look good because the health of your business is more important than one person's feelings or ego. This also ensures there are no surprises regarding what needs to be done by someone else; everyone knows what is expected of them and how long they have until their next review. That allows people to plan instead of getting stuck with something at the last minute and scrambling around looking for help or trying desperately not to let anyone down.

Support your team

You must do what you can to support your team. For example, if your employees aren't comfortable giving you feedback (or fear they might offend you), try encouraging more interaction between them and you. Encourage lunch or after-work get-togethers with each other and make sure they feel comfortable sharing their ideas with you—or even each other. If team members know how valuable their work is, they'll be happier at work and more likely to stick around. Create an environment where communication is open and encouraged; those who feel supported by their employer are generally much happier employees who see themselves working there long term. That leads to greater employee retention, saving you money in turnover costs and keeping the business strong. Also, when your employees are happy at work, they will be much more productive than when they are not! In short: happy employees equal a stronger business.

Have clear guidelines

While employees need a certain level of freedom and autonomy at work, it's also important that you set firm guidelines and standards. Clear instructions help employees focus on their tasks and understand their expectations. So don't be afraid to set rules; make sure you explain them clearly so everyone knows how they should operate while on your team. Clear rules can increase employee satisfaction because they will know what is expected of them. In addition, when employees know what's required of them, they are more likely to give you good feedback about how things could be improved within your business. Clear guidelines will also make it easier to spot when someone isn't doing their job properly or may not be right for your company culture. If someone isn't performing well or following protocol, you can deal with these issues sooner rather than later. Of course, letting people go shouldn't come as a surprise – but having clear expectations will allow you to do so quickly and easily when necessary.

Chapter 6

The Challenges- What Can Separate Us from our Valued Team

Unwillingness to build a hybrid or remote team

There's a common misconception among startup owners that to have a successful company; one needs to have all their employees under one roof in an office setting, preferably with complimentary coffee and soft drinks on tap. However, this notion isn't true, and the statistics back it up. The great thing about virtual teams is that we can hire from anywhere in the world! We can add freelance service providers from apps like Fiverr and Upwork as a part of our team, if you are stuck in the old mindset of having your team in the office, this will lead to a significant challenge.

How Has Remote Work Impacted Our Business?

There are many reasons, but it ultimately comes down to respect and trust. Remote workers need structure, and good communication like their office-based colleagues do. The difference is that they need these things differently. When you respect your employees and treat them well as professionals, you earn their trust over time, leading them to do great work for you, making your business even more successful. And so on! What we've found works best with remote teams combines work when and where you want with clear accountability structures and expectations. If people know what they should be working on and what sort of output to expect from them each week, then there's no reason why they can't be incredibly productive from wherever they choose to work. That said, some environments are better than others for getting focused work done.

What Can My Company Achieve by Building a Hybrid or Remote Team?

No matter your industry, these days, there is no shortage of high-quality developers, software engineers, and product managers available. What you can't find easily are talented individuals who are passionate about their work and care about your company's core mission and values. But that doesn't mean you can't find them! What if you could attract these people by building a full-time team? Enter Hybrid Teams. By creating a virtual office space, you have access to talent worldwide. In fact, according to Fast Company magazine, 46% of employees say they would take a 10% pay cut in exchange for working remotely. This means they value flexible schedules more than traditional working hours! Additionally, 59% said they would be willing to travel as long as they could stay connected and productive while away from home. So if attracting top talent and enabling collaboration with colleagues around the globe sounds appealing, starting up a virtual office might be right for your business.

Why Aren't We Moving Faster?

The common refrain we hear from business leaders is that they don't have enough information to make decisions. Even if you hire great people and set them up with technology, there's always a chance they won't be able to figure out what to do next on their own. The only way around that is by ensuring your teams are moving quickly and getting more things done quickly. How? By spending time planning their days instead of doing it for them. A few simple steps can make your employees happier and better at what they do —if you don't trust them enough, it may be time to reconsider hiring remote workers. If you want to get more work done faster without sacrificing quality, try turning to contractors in a different city or country who can bring fresh perspectives. Hiring someone new is always risky, but investing in an experienced virtual assistant can save your company time and money while freeing up valuable internal resources. Virtual assistants have proven track records of delivering high-quality work in specific fields. Investing in a good one will ensure you never lose another minute searching for answers online or coordinating between different departments.

How Will You Accomplish It?

There are many benefits to working with others, regardless of location. But for one reason or another, our human natures can get in our way and hold us back from making that happen. We may not have great ideas on how we can make it work, fear that people won't take our directions seriously because they aren't face-to-face with us all day long, or wonder if we need more experience on our end before heading down such a path. It's enough doubt and negativity to stop anyone in their tracks! But there are also significant benefits of bringing together diverse skill sets and environments where folks can work remotely - you have the know-how. If you're having trouble convincing your boss (or yourself) that hiring remote workers is a good idea, here are some tips on making your case.

Tips & Tricks from Others in This Space

Remember who you're trying to reach when deciding if a specific hire is worth it. For example, it may be tempting to snag that ultra-qualified Java expert from down south familiar with all your company's competitors, but do they know much about your industry and how things operate in your area? If not, there may be an equally talented candidate right down the street who already knows your customer base and whose skills translate just as well. And then ask yourself—are you going to force them (or worse, bring them into an office setting where they won't mesh), or are you going to give them all their work remotely so they can work in whatever environment best suits their needs?

The challenges of having a hybrid or remote team

Having a remote team can be a massive asset to your business, but it also comes with its share of challenges. For example, working across time zones and multiple cultures can create difficulties when you need to collaborate with your employees. In addition, finding the right tools to keep everyone on the same page regarding communication and workflow management can be challenging. This content will introduce you to the top five challenges of having a remote team, along with ideas and suggestions for overcoming them to have a robust and well-rounded team of virtual workers.

Communication

There are two factors to consider when working with remote employees. First, you must ensure everyone has equal access to resources and information. For example, all employees need direct access to their software, regardless of location. Second, your communication must be open and honest at all times. You can achieve transparency by encouraging a sense of personal connection between all team members through regular meetings or group chats. To minimize miscommunication, your team should have clearly defined roles and an established process for sharing important information throughout every stage of development (e.g., sprint planning meetings). By facilitating clear communication on both an individual and group level, you ensure everyone on your team is up-to-date on what's happening.

Collaboration

Collaboration is one of your biggest challenges. To manage the cooperation between remote employees, you'll need to ensure your company's communication tools are up to snuff. A simple IM system won't cut it; instead, find a project management tool that offers file sharing and group messaging capabilities. This will help keep all conversations on-topic and prevent important messages from being overlooked or accidentally ignored. You may also want to use video conferencing to communicate in real-time via face-to-face meetings; making yourself available for regular conference calls allows people thousands of miles apart to feel like they're in adjacent cubicles. And if you have an extensive team, consider hiring someone to act as a virtual office manager. They can handle employee scheduling and oversee other logistical concerns (like ordering supplies), so everyone else can focus on their jobs.

Accountability

If you have employees that aren't in-office, it's easy for them to feel like they can disappear. However, if your remote team doesn't interact regularly, you risk falling behind and dealing with unanticipated issues when everyone does meet up. Schedule weekly or monthly calls or meetings with each remote employee so you all stay on track. You could also set up goals (like reaching out to new clients) and monitor their progress as a group; that way, you can help hold each other accountable and reach business objectives together, no matter where in the world you are.

Staying honest about what tasks need to be done and who is responsible for them is another challenge of managing a remote team. The good news is that several tools are available to help—from software that assigns tasks and projects with due dates and sends reminders through project management apps to even full-fledged time tracking services designed specifically for freelancers. Use what works best for your needs, but don't overlook accountability! It helps keep projects on schedule and ensures no one gets left behind if they don't take the initiative themselves.

Motivation

Remote workers need extra motivation and accountability even with no manager to drive them and no colleagues at their elbow. For example, to get work done, you have to manage your time effectively and stay on task, which is more complicated than it sounds. Studies show that every hour spent telecommuting results in one fewer hour of work accomplished. A key reason for these results is boredom: Remote workers often stare out into space as they mindlessly open up new tabs, check Facebook—and then feel guilty about wasted time. As a result, many employees struggle to complete even basic tasks during their off-hours. To solve this problem, create an action plan for each employee (including yourself) outlining how many hours per week they should be working remotely.

Time management

Let's say you want to finish two tasks in one day. The first task will take four hours, and the second will take 10. If you spread those tasks evenly throughout your workday, you'll spend six hours working on things not associated with your job. If you can find a way to limit distractions and maximize focus during work hours, it's possible to get more done without having to sacrifice sleep or social life. You may experiment with different strategies until you find what works best. But if you don't manage your time effectively, even if you manage to hire top talent from around the world, they won't be able to help much because they'll be too busy trying to figure out how to balance their lives and jobs. So when hiring remote workers, make sure to ask about their time-management skills.

Summary

In this book, James H. Bradshaw talks about what many entrepreneurs who want success do not realize: it's one thing to get a team but quite another thing when you don't manage your team correctly. Many entrepreneurs try to get by on their own, and then, when they find out how much more effective teams are than going solo, they need to take care that they are doing everything right in managing that team so as not to lose their best people. They need to make sure that there is no resentment or backstabbing, or any other negative feelings between themselves and their teammates. They also have to ensure that everyone understands what is expected of them, including how many hours per week will be spent at work (and why), what benefits are available (if any), etc. The point is, there's much more involved in getting a team up and running than simply hiring someone. Once you have hired someone, you have to set up an environment where everyone feels valued and appreciated while still being productive without creating resentment among those working for you. That's where entrepreneur James H. Bradshaw comes in with his new book Entrepreneurs Building Your Teams the Way You Want them to Make Your Business More Productive Than Ever!

Conclusion

You've just read Entrepreneurs Building Your Teams the Way You Want them to Make Your Business More Productive Than Ever! You can confidently say, I'm ready to apply these principles in my business! But before you put the book down, here are a few additional resources that you may find helpful as you transition into your new business-building mindset.

Too many entrepreneurs are stuck in their success rut and not building their teams properly to make their business more productive. Learn some new and proven ways how you can build your dream team so that you'll stay busy, profitable, and happy while living life on your terms. By implementing these tips, you'll start living a life beyond goals. The book was developed by a serial entrepreneur who has taught these strategies to others who have become successful. With over two decades of experience as an entrepreneur, he has seen what works for him and what doesn't for him when it comes down to selecting, mentoring, and hiring his dream team. He's also learned how to develop leaders within his organization and help them reach their full potential. As a result, he knows exactly what other entrepreneurs need to do if they want to achieve similar results. So, if you want to be successful like never before, read Entrepreneurs Building Your Teams the Way You Want them to Make Your Business More Productive Than Ever! Now! This is one step-by-step guide you won't want to miss out on. It will give you everything you need to build your dream team today. Let him help put more money in your pocket each month and show you how much easier it is to scale once you have a good team working for you instead of against you!

This book is designed to teach any entrepreneur (even beginners) everything they need to know about building high-performance teams with proven methods and tactics. It is written so people can build teams and make their businesses run as smoothly as possible.

This book is not just for entrepreneurs but all business owners, small or large; anyone with a dream or goal can benefit from reading and applying some of these techniques. It's written in plain English without complicated jargon so that anyone can understand it. It's a simple step-by-step guide on building your team using common sense and proven methods. It will help you avoid mistakes most new entrepreneurs make when building their team and show you how to immediately get your business running smoothly. After reading this book, we hope you can take your business to another level, increase productivity, eliminate stress and keep more money in your pocket.

The tools you have learned from Entrepreneurs Building Your Teams the Way You Want them to Make Your Business More Productive Than Ever! Help you get started and build a sustainable business. Use them. Start small, think big, and do it right the first time. But remember, you will sometimes fail—just don't let that stop you from trying again because that is how we learn and grow. Never give up! Never surrender!!!

Saying Thank You for taking your valuable time to read this book! We hope you enjoyed it as much as we did while writing it. Stay tuned for more awesome books by James H. Bradshaw coming soon. Until then, Good Luck and Happy Startup!!

References

Gardner, H. (1983). Frames of mind: the theory of multiple intelligences. Basic books.

Gallup, Inc. (2020). How to improve employee engagement in the workplace. https://www.gallup.com/workplace/285674/improve-employee-engagement-workplace.aspx

Seligman, M. (2011). PERMA - A well-being theory. Free press.

Bradshaw, K.D. (2018). In search of the solitude streams paperback. CreateSpace independent publishing platform.

Fogg, B.J. (2019). Tiny habits: the small changes that change everything. https://bit.ly/Tiny-Habits-Changes-Change-Everything

Hess, T. (2007). Understanding a Company's Culture. https://www.thebalancecareers.com/company-culture-2275155

Sutton, R.I. (2010). Good Boss, Bad Boss: How to Be the Best and Survive The Worst. Business plus.

Grant, A. (2013). Give and Take : Why Helping Others Drives Our Success. Penguin Books

www.ingramcontent.com/pod-product-compliance
Lightning Source LLC
Chambersburg PA
CBHW062116220526
45471CB00010B/3752